Heart on a String

Heart on a String

poems
Tom Boswell

GRAYSON BOOKS
West Hartford, Connecticut
www.graysonbooks.com

Heart on a String
copyright © 2020 by Tom Boswell
Published by Grayson Books
West Hartford, Connecticut
ISBN: 978-1-7335568-5-9
Library of Congress Control Number: 2020915381

Book & cover design: Cindy Stewart
Cover photo: iStock.com/fortise
Author photo: Aaron Bos-Wahl

Advance Praise for *Heart on a String*

Tom Boswell's *Heart on a String* is a funny, tender, no-nonsense look at serious relationships that finally come to an end. The poems here are like the delicate touch-me-not that propagates when the flower, held by the most tenuous stem, breaks and spills its seed. Wearing their hearts on such a delicate string, these poems help us understand the connections and disconnections of love. And they help us, as all the best poems do, to see the familiar world less familiarly, see the "miracle in the mundane."
—Robert Cording, author of *Walking with Ruskin*

In *Heart on a String*, Tom Boswell shows himself to be a highly articulate translator of the natural world, and a perceptive narrator of his own journey down the decades. It's a book in which a bucolic poem about fishing, for example, will suddenly morph into an action-shot of leaping carp, *hurling themselves up on the concrete skirt of the dam…with a reckless and resolute grace."* A bit further on, a starry sky turns to *embers that burned bright / with savage fury / just a billion years ago*. But perhaps most impressive of all are Boswell's moving personal stories of love and mortality, which simply do not lend themselves to paraphrase—but will take the reader's breath away.
—Marilyn L. Taylor, Wisconsin Poet Laureate Emeritus

Tom Boswell opens wide the spaces no one else even sees. His images astound and expand even as the lines are cast in your direction, and you are caught. The title of the poem "In the English Language There Is Only One Word for Dream" alone should trip you in your tracks, but the lines, double-edged and keen, part the world and wake you to the way words can really work: "the doctors have unclogged, once more, the pathway to my heart." And you should be in a hurry, too, to read "If I Had Gone to Church" for the sheer glory of the kingdom everyone else but Tom missed on Sunday morning. Read, my friends, read these words that will refresh your eyes, swell your heart, and lighten your head with sun and wonder.

—Eric Paul Shaffer, author of *Even Further West*

Acknowledgements

Atlanta Review: Government in a Box
Blue Earth Review: River City; The Catalpa in June
Clare Literary Journal: El Fuego; The Real Story
The Dos Passos Review: Country Commute
Glass Mountain: After Reading the First Poem in the Literary Journal…
The Lascaux Prize: Leaving the Garden
Local News: Poetry About Small Towns: The Rental Next Door
the minnesota review: Young Americans Dressed in Black
Peninsula Pulse: In the English Language There Is Only One Word…
Poet Lore: On the Phone; Snapshots from Another Time
PoetryPort: The Devil's Grandmother; Domestic Bliss
Potomac Review: Summertime
Rattle: Harvesting the Carrots
Sojourn: The Carp at Kiel
Two Thirds North: If I Had Gone to Church
Wisconsin Academy Review: Country Graveyard
Wisconsin People & Ideas: My Lover's Braids

Contents

Heart of Glass
Harvesting the Carrots	13
Summertime	15
Dodder	16
My Lover's Braids	17
Heart on a String	18
Domestic Bliss	19
On the Phone	22

River Towns and Country Roads
River City	25
Country Commute	27
Country Graveyard	28
Spring Green	30
Arsenal Island	32
The Carp at Kiel	34

Neighbors
Nothing Happens Here	37
The Rental Next Door	39
The Neighbor	41
There's a Cross at the Edge of Town	42
The Catalpa in June	44
All Hallows' Eve	45
The Serviceberry	47

Life in the Driftless
Meditation While Cutting Buckwheat	51
Crows	53
Picking Apples	54
The Butterfly Does Yoga	55
November Woods	56

Government in a Box
Cold Day in November	61
The Real Story	62
My God is Greater Than Your God	63
Young Americans Dressed in Black	65
El Fuego	67
Government in a Box	68

Snapshots from Another Time
Snapshots from Another Time   73

The Devil's Grandmother
If I Had Gone to Church   81
Leftovers   82
Table Manners   84
In the English Language There Is Only One Word for Dream   85
Leaving the Garden   86
After Reading the First Poem in the Literary Journal, I Stop to Contemplate Life and Death   88
The Devil's Grandmother   90

About the Author   91

Heart of Glass

Harvesting the Carrots

Ten years later, when it was finally over,
    she confessed she had fallen in love
    with me that late autumn afternoon
    while I squatted, my back to her,
    harvesting the carrots.

My eyes were fixed on the carrot tops, ferny green
    filigree promising thick scarlet roots
    burrowed in the soil, so I failed to notice
    if she changed that moment—her face,
    her eyes, the way she walked—

When this thing she later called love swept
    over her. I do remember that the corn
    was behind us, and how she turned then
    to photograph it as I tore out carrots
    and tossed them in a willow basket.

I never understood what she saw in this garden
    she hadn't worked, or in the ravaged corn
    she'd make into a photo to hang on a gallery
    wall, or how these things she hardly knew
    could stir such deep emotions, but

I've come to trust the way the bandit coon craves
    the corn, something pure and simple, lacking
    pretense. The photograph was one of those
    soft-focus works of hers you could
    hang any which way and still

See something to satisfy you, so long as you
    were not hungry for corn. There was mullein,
    goldenrod and bergamot still in bloom,
    and the *wild* carrot, Queen Anne's Lace,
    which she claimed to love as well.

I teased her, called it a wanton weed, useless
    renegade from overseas, but showed her,
    as if it was a secret shared by just us two,

　　　　the solitary purple blossom shuddering
　　　　like a heart at the center of each bouquet.

Gather enough of these over a summer, I said,
　　　　and you can dye something—a skirt or shirt
　　　　perhaps—a dark hue like the stain
　　　　of memory, a thing of beauty and utility.
　　　　At least until the color fades.

Summertime

On my way to work
I'm thinking about lost love
and love that never was
and a new love
that just came around the corner
and the radio is playing
Summertime and I want to cry
when I hear the sax
pliant and plaintive
and full of yearning and regret
but I have to keep myself
together because I'm looking
at nine hours taking care
of the old man with dementia
and need to pretend
to be more present than he
though it's summertime
and it hasn't rained in three months
and I want nothing more
nor less than to slip
out of my mind for a while—
like those people who've learned
how to float above their bodies—
not to lose it
forever, mind you, like
the old man, just long enough
to really miss it,
like a lost love
or a hard rain
or a good cry.

Dodder

glistened in the crisp September
light, a frenzy of copper snakes,
twisting and twining among
the jewelweed
and other meadow plants.

You found it amusing—
even without its peculiar
name which I remembered
much later—

and I loved the way you laughed
at this joke of a plant
and the way you would twist and turn
through your fingers
your long golden hair
still moist from the shower.

But, as it played out
those bright clear autumn
mornings, you were the
jewelweed—the *touch-me-not*—
the delicate sunburnt blossoms,
each with a tear-drop of dew
in the early meadow mist,
and I—the other one—the leafless
interloper with the funny
forgettable name, and suckers
hoping in vain to feed off
your green green leaves.

My Lover's Braids

When my last lover
                left
she left her long brown braids
in the dresser drawer

so I hung them from the
                garden fence
to scare the deer away.

Heart on a String

She gave me a little heart
of glass, on a string, saying
I could hang it in the window
and let the sun shine through.
It was so...perfect, I thought,
unlike our love...It ought

to be a lopsided heart,
like the leaf of the basswood,
or the lolling lopsided moon,
not yet full and pristine tonight,
resembling a smashed peach
as it slips so tentatively
from behind the dark hills.

Domestic Bliss

1.
*This town is way too tidy,
too tedious*, she protests.
Just the yap of a dog
next door, *thank God for that*.
Boxes still scattered
on the floor, she laments
the loss of city life:
whine and spew of traffic,
sporadic gunshots
late at night.

Then the man
in the elegant Victorian
across the street
shatters the godawful quiet,
beating his young wife,
who runs into the street
in her negligee as neighbors
dutifully call the cops.

She sighs with relief
and wonders
where to plug the toaster.

2.
He remembers helping her
move to Chicago, where she
never hung one picture
on the white apartment walls.
Now here they are, together,
in this tame universe
between city and farm.

3.
He navigates the damp jungle
of her clothes—bras, panties,
socks—dangling like serpents
from hooks, racks and chairs,

pictures himself an explorer
on a strange new continent.

4.
When they saw each other
weekends, they read poems
out loud in bed. Now they peruse
pamphlets from the hardware
and Farm & Fleet, pointing
out which paint is cheapest
and the best deal
on a toilet plunger.

When they walk uptown,
they pass Church Street, with its
churches, School Street, with its
school, and Liberty, with its library
and post office. He frets
he may be trapped inside
a Norman Rockwell painting.

5.
One day she grabs a magnet
and posts a flyer titled
Holy Relationships
on the side of the fridge,
like Martin Luther
nailing his treatise
to the cathedral door.

But next to it is the list
of Sunday chores: caulk
the sink, grout around the tub,
buy a mousetrap
or find a cat.

6.
She bought a book
on tantric sex but fell
asleep in her sweats,
the book spread open

on her chest like a butterfly
drying its wings.

He looks at her sweet, tired
face, her mussed hair, and reflects
on the modest, sometimes messy
nest they are making together—
wattle of twigs and twine, hope
and habit, dreams and schemes
and fear, and thinks—perhaps
they will be happy here.

On the Phone

we talked about what you
had seen on TV and what
I had heard on the radio
and which candidate
was likely to do the least
damage to the common wealth
and what we both might do
to earn a living and my
mother's health and would
it rain again this week
and where we might live
and why a letter was better
than email but was it worth
the wait but I forgot
to tell you that the phoebe
who late this spring
had built her nest
above the kitchen window
was still there and had
had her babies
and how I first heard
their eager chatter and then
saw them their three young
mouths stretching
like summer daylilies
toward paradise.

River Towns and Country Roads

River City

The statue of Mary
holds her head
in her hands

while snakes bask
on the steaming street
in front of the church.

Strange immense trees
on the bluffs thrust
their arms out like sleepwalkers
and squirrels scampering
in their shade
are dark as devils.

Just before dusk, locusts
begin to hum
and the trees pulsate
like some primordial power line.

The sluggish river lingers
and sulks. A big paddleboat
is moored to the dock, glittering
like a tawdry carnival.
Tourists and townsfolk, pockets
full of cash, parade on board
complacent as beef cattle.

Fish leap
from the water
as if trying to become
some new creature
or enter another life.
Bodies

float downstream
all day
but no one has a pole
to fish them out.
On an island

close to shore
blackbirds swarm
in the briars
and young women,
lips moist with worry,
wait in the woods
for the married men
to come.

Trains tremble by
all night
on the tracks by the river.
Possum lurk in the alleys
like winos, and old men
dressed in black
sit alone in their bedrooms
late into the sweltering
night, dreaming
of burning witches
once again.

Country Commute

Midsummer morning, driving along
this country highway, late for work
again. Already it's too warm
for a tie.

Queen Anne's Lace rims the road
and chicory and ditch lilies blaze
in blue and orange. I consider

tidy fields of corn and beans,
spotted mares huddled in a pasture
beneath a copse of oaks, and a llama,

recently shorn, wearing a philosopher's grin.
It is that time again when I wish not
to be working, to have my sentence commuted,

to be free of worry forever, like I imagine
this old man to be, riding his rickety
three-wheel bike through this one-stop-sign

town, knobby knees pumping the pedals
like rusty pistons, one of those big rearview
mirrors clamped to the handlebars so he can see

everything he is leaving behind.

Country Graveyard

On the truck radio someone
        is singing about a free rambling

no-strings-attached sort of love
        as I drive past a country

graveyard where an old man on a sit-
        down mower is wending his way

betwixt and between the flowers
        and flags and tombstones

so the parson and families and cemetery
        committee can rest assured

that on his watch, this steamy summer
        day, no grass will grow

beneath the feet of these discarded
        souls. Why, I don't know, but

now I think of cowboy boots
        stomping on a bare wood floor,

people prancing round and round,
        the face of a woman,

and Janis wailing on and on
        about how freedom's just another

word for nothin' left to lose
        and the Jesuit who said love

is to be found only in fearlessness
        but I fear every choice

is another spoonful of death
        and wonder how much more

I need to lose or is it only
         somewhere way up yonder,

well beyond this country boneyard,
         that freedom and love finally lock

arms in a fierce and lasting embrace.

Spring Green

So there he lay under an apple tree nursing
        his hurt just half-drunk
musing with these throbbing strangers

this swarm of stars wondering how long
        each needs to burn itself
into oblivion while up the hill is the country inn

where he had sat with her and her friends
        downing beers flirting
as the jester from the city amused tourists

and country folk for a fool's fee. She was
        an artist and a dancer
he'd met earlier that day but she excused herself

for a moment and never returned and now
        here he wakes to sounds
of laughter wafting thru open windows weaving

with the chatter of crickets. He had hoped these
        serene rolling hills these lush
valleys might heal harsh city scars bring peace

but the sharp lines of her face scraped like a scalpel
        across old wounds
he never learned to mask. She must have known

there was nothing to be gained here so he doesn't
        blame her it was
Adam after all plucked that apple on his own

restless even then wanting more than Eden
        could provide though God
saw it all was good but they also say He brooded

perhaps even got bored with His handiwork
        and what accounts
for these damn mosquitoes if it was all so good?

She had studied him with probing artist's eyes
        as if taking notes
for a charcoal sketch and perhaps he only wanted

her to package in a poem wrap her up in neat ribbons
        of rhythm and rhyme
but what's so bad with that? Much later he'll begin

to learn the garden's not past or future
        and demons and saints
both dwell together there but for now he stumbles

from his rumpled bed beneath the tree forsaking
        both the cunning clown
and the woman. He races his car toward the river.

He brakes the car just shy of the water's edge
        where many others have lost
their way. The two-faced jester will die instead,

crumpled body found like a hapless doe on the dark
        country road. He doesn't dare
to ask what the coroner uncovered whether

pain or peace or hollowness beneath the mask.

Arsenal Island

Today we come on bikes—
as if to elude the sentries—
to this strange island floating

like an ancient sturgeon
in this turbid river
by the sleeping cities.

We come to green grass
and granite tombstones
that mark the sleeping soldiers

and lie in the grass,
faces slewed like flowers
on long stems toward

the summer sun. We kiss
for the first time, and then
again, the steel guns still.

They say that freed slaves
guarded rebel soldiers
here during the war.

You rest your head on my
outstretched arm and I listen
to you softly breathing.

The guns are still, just
the stretching trees and grass
and graves and brooding river

with its dark memories
of slaves and war and loss.
We both have sons and long

to teach them what arms are for
but our hearts are guarded.
I try to imagine a love

brave and strong and hot
enough to melt steel
but fear is what I feel.

We rise and mount our bikes
and take the bridge back
to the city. I pursue

you, up the steep hills, lungs
and heart burning like a foundry
in the sultry summer evening.

The Carp at Kiel

As the summer day waned into evening,
I stopped for ice cream in Kiel, then wandered
down to the old mill, wondering
what might be biting. There were two fishermen—

biker types in leather with skull-and-crossbones
earrings— ready to try their luck elsewhere,
and a boy on a bike, fishing rod across the handlebars,
who had had no luck upstream. Only flies

and mosquitoes biting. But there were carp,
an endless parade of them, flinging themselves
at the dam as if storming a fortress!
One by one they leapt out of the roily water,

a righteous frenzy of fins, scales and light flashing
in the rapids, fighting the raging force of the river
after a month of relentless rain. The most defiant
fish hurled themselves up on the concrete skirt

of the dam, where they skimmed and slid
against the rush of water before slipping
back into the hurly-burly below.
Watching each carp take a turn, I thought

of that saying from the Seventies about how a woman
needs a man like a fish needs a bicycle, and then I wished
you had been here—for all those times we almost
lose faith—to see those stubborn fish in their solitary

and spectacular leaps, looking like they were learning
to ride unicycles, rehearsing for the summer circus.
They didn't seem ridiculous, after all, and it struck me
that, if those carp could find purpose in this dogged

diversion, performing that queer dance with a
reckless and resolute grace, then there was reason
to believe we could find our love
a compelling if not altogether practical thing.

Neighbors

Nothing Happens Here

It's just a quiet little town
surrounded by soybeans and corn.
A mile out the main road
near the farm that sells eggs
with the sign *Got Milk?* painted
on the old concrete silo,
and with the squat little cemetery
just to the west,
sits a nondescript house. If you passed
it by on your way to someplace else,
you wouldn't even notice it, were it not
for the plastic pumpkins festooned
on the porch railing, since
it's nearly Halloween.

The children don't come out this far
for tricks and treats, and nowadays
their parents tag along,
even in town. But one girl, just out
of high school, answers an ad
on the internet and a man
picks her up in the city and brings her back
to this too-ordinary-looking house
he rents from a farmer down the road.
He has his five-month old daughter,
like an after-thought, along
for the ride. It's not clear if the girl
has come for drugs or sex or just money,
but by morning she is dead.

So the man drives to the hardware store
on the edge of town for a shovel
and some kerosene, returns to his house
and digs a hole–what neighbors call
a burn pit–in the back yard.

He hauls her body out in a blanket
and stashes it under his pickup
till he has the fire burning well.

Then he fetches the body from under
the truck and puts it on the pyre.

It's a spirited fire–neighbors drive by
and wave, and later, one claims the flames
were eight feet high–and after a while
his fiancée, (who must have been at work
in the city), returns and he sends her
to the grocery store in town
to buy the stuff for making 'smores
while he faithfully tends the fire,
adding brush as needed.

I suppose everyone here will have their own
theory about this loony campfire cook-out:
Some will say it was to ease suspicion
of neighbors or his bride-to-be. Or
to smother the god-awful stench
with chocolate and marshmallows, or
just so as not to waste a good fire.
Others will insist the whole 'smores thing
was just hear-say or something the TV news
in the city added to spice up the story,
to make our evil out here seem less paltry.

When the police tape comes down, some people
will surely place flowers and things near the porch,
where the plastic pumpkins had been.
Others will call for *closure*.
That's what we do these days,
when something like this happens.

The Rental Next Door

It's a ramshackle place,
its only purpose to make money
for its owner, like a whore
for her pimp.

Tenants come and go. Most
I never get to know.

Once a man moved in
for a while. I think he thought
his stay would be short.
He would go some day, when
his wife wanted him back.

Sometimes his son came to visit
and the two of them would practice
with a bow and arrows
in the back yard. They seemed so serious,
as if it were much more than play.

They placed a target back near
the woods but the son's arrows
often went astray, as if shot
by a blind or drunken cupid.
The man was patient, taking pains
to teach the son how to nock
the arrow in the string,
pull, aim and let it fly.

The man must have had a gun
because he was a deputy sheriff
in the city nearby, but I suppose
that would have been too easy.
There was the matter of the son
and the life insurance policy.

One week the house next door
sat quiet, except for the wind
rattling the dangling drainpipes,
and then came the story

in the paper about how his car
had swerved across the center line
on his way home from work
and hit a semi straight on.
The story didn't say, but rumors
were his wife had found
herself another lover.

Later she came and collected
all the stuff from the upper flat,
hauled some away in a truck,
but tossed most on the curb
for the neighbors to pick through
like crows pecking for their lunch.
There wasn't much of value to be had.
I did see the bow and a quiver
full of arrows buried under a broken
wooden chair, but something said
to me it was better left alone.

The Neighbor

There goes my neighbor again,
out walking his little white dog
in the listless rain.

His hair is turning white
as the dog's, which means
he is getting older. Which means
I must be getting older too.

He has some kind of cancer,
he told me recently, but
that does not deter me
from asking him to lend a hand
when I have some heavy work to do.

He pauses, out in the languid rain,
or maybe it's the dog that pauses
first, needing to pee. No matter.
They both pause and look around

as if they are lost for a moment,
or maybe they are just not
in a hurry, having both made peace
with relentless time, and then
they walk on in the lackluster rain.

There's a Cross at the Edge of Town

Those people who publish
the weekly paper
put up an imposing wooden cross
at the edge of town
just before Good Friday.

We thought they'd take it down
after Easter but it's still there…

My lover, who's Jewish,
cringes when we pass it by

and the road to the city
is littered with little white crosses,
an invasive species
lacking natural predators.

They mark all the places
people died while rushing
to work in the morning
or returning home at the end
of the day. One for the woman
who collided with a semi
while trying to pass a tractor,
another for the young girl
on a bike sideswiped by an SUV,
three teens joyriding late at night,
the man who swerved to avoid
a deer and rolled his car into a ravine…

In that other empire
long ago, people didn't die
in cars like caged creatures.
Rather they were hammered
to crosses perched on hilltops,
thousands upon thousands
writhing on trees of death
for the more docile subjects
to see, and only one
whose name we still recall.

Bandits, zealots, insurrectionists
they called them then,
victims of state terror, a naked
warning to others not to follow
these wayward Jews hanging
all over the empire, skulls
littering the hillsides like rubble.

Now here we are, forced
to pass this ominous cross
on our way out of town.
We are not certain what message
they mean to send, these people
who put it here, who put out
the weekly paper, but we doubt
it is good news.

The Catalpa in June

It's all so fast, so fleeting, so perverse
the way the Catalpa blooms, then shrugs off
its profligate white bouquets each June.

Soon they fill the lawn, to be followed
later by the long pods resembling abandoned
snake skins, then finally the enormous

heart-shaped leaves. All this beauty spent,
relinquished, for what? Leaving for work,
I back my car onto the street, marveling

at all this wanton waste. On the sidewalk
is a woman of indeterminate age, hair
draggled like scraggly weeds, an infant

clinging to her hip. At her side, a girl
with long, dark, luxurious hair. She is beautiful.
Her eyes catch mine, then look away.

This family—I surmise—lives in one of these
shabby duplexes with bare wood and tattered
tarpaper scattered among the Victorians.

The girl could be a model or a debutante,
if only she came from money. But money
doesn't grow on trees. Only white flowers

that fade, then fall, too fast, each June.

All Hallows' Eve

Tonight marks the birth of the year's dark half
and there's a party just outside of town
at an old farmhouse. Teen-age children

are out back playing *Truth or Dare*. There's
a garden swing, bonfire, and tub of apples.
Horses graze in the distance, near the pond.

I'm dressed in black and wearing a ghoulish
rubber mask with long black straggly hair.
My partner has a necklace of garlic hanging

from her neck to ward off vampires. Grown-ups
are in the kitchen, chatting about church, good
priests and bad ones, while chewing chips

and toasted pumpkin seeds. My plan is not
to take the mask off till the sun sets—keep
everyone guessing—though most are strangers.

Then the man of the house leads us
from kitchen to living room. The farmhouse
is filled with jack-o-lanterns and black cats,

goblins, ghosts, spiders, skeletons and bats.
This is the fifteenth party, notes the father.
We had the first when he was just one.

He talks softly about his son, the youngest one,
who isn't there. *Something wasn't right*,
he says, *was never quite right with him.*

Orange lights are blinking furiously and no,
I'm not mad, there's even the sound
of a thumping heart. These folks have thought

of everything. *It was his favorite holiday*, the father
says about the son, and now I wonder
if we should have come, had we known. I'm feeling

hot and foolish but it's too late to remove
the mask and the heart is beating louder
from the speakers in every corner of the room

and I hear him mutter something about the pond,
this man whose face is much too naked
this holiday when ancestors are honored

and invited in, this evening when the space
between two worlds grows thin. But the time
has been too brief, the heart beats on malevolently

and the father can't disguise his grief. Did I
mention? The mother's a witch, but broom-less
as she haunts the kitchen, a familiar spirit

of domesticity and death, but she goes outside
more often than necessary to check
on the children, make sure they don't wander

too near the pond. Soon it will be dark.

The Serviceberry

You had planned, in your practical, persistent
English manner, that it would be spring
when we visited your charming country estate.
The same way—I imagine—that you planned
this house and gardens resting on the last moraine
of the last glacier. But it was cold that day,
the wind still biting and blustery, the Serviceberry—
your prized possession—still hesitant to bloom.

You had a husband of sixty years who needed
cheering, his surgery scheduled for week's end,
so you hid your worry while he, in his practical
English way, wrote his epitaph. After brunch,
we braved the wind and walked the hilly land,
you the polite but proud docent pointing out
each native shrub and flower, sometimes
searching for its name like someone
looking for a light switch in a dark room.

I must confess I envied you again, that day,
for all those living things that seemed to do
your bidding, but now I think you found
your bliss in creating, not controlling.
Others say you could not suffer fools, and so
I feel you would not fool yourself to think
we can claim these neat kingdoms we fashion
any more than we can dicker with death.

How I despise it when obit writers or TV pundits
remark that so-and-so's was an *untimely* death!
Scripture says there's a time for everything
but whose death is ever timely? Not now,
when fickle spring comes creeping in at last,
when everything is waking and your Serviceberry
explodes with clusters of white blossoms.

Your husband was still healing in the hospital
when you fell, that night. Found the next morning,
the first of May, by your daughter. What caused

the fall–heart attack or stroke–is anybody's guess,
but the hypothesis is you died of hypothermia.
You were lying with your head by the bleeding hearts.

No, let's not make those innocent flowers
a bloody metaphor. It is what it is.
A metaphor means *to carry over*
and every gardener knows nothing stays put
where it's planted, no matter how precisely
planned. You might just as easily have taken
your final sleep by the maidenhair fern,
the irises or hostas, or even the Serviceberry.

The tree claims so many names. *Serviceberry*,
they say, because years ago impatient couples
would wait out the long, cold mountain winters
until the preacher who rode the circuit
would arrive to conduct wedding services…
which was when the dirt roads were dry enough
to traverse in horse and buggy…which was when
the tree began to bloom. There's also *shadbush*
or *shadblow*, and *Juneberry* because that's the month

the petite berries ripen to blue. The songbirds
love them but I imagine you managed to pick
some first and baked a cobbler for your husband
and friends. Who will harvest the berries this year
or would you be content to leave them for the birds?
Will the frogs still be chattering in your ponds?
What would the wild lilies you planted, if they
could open their yellow throats and speak,
utter at this most untimely time
when once again all the world is bursting alive?

Life in the Driftless

Meditation While Cutting Buckwheat

I'm hacking down buckwheat
with the rusty old scythe

trying to spare the milkweed
for the monarchs

like a merciful god. Later
I'll toss white-blossomed

stems on the compost heap
and stir it like stew to turn

dying life into new. Still
planning to sow winter rye

but I'm breathing hard.

This tool could have been a golf club
if I'd picked a simpler path.

I could die on a well-tended fairway
struck down by lightning

or a heart attack. A grim thought.
I swing the scythe in a jerky arc

and think of Leopold who died
fighting a brush fire the year

I was born and his student
Jim Zim cut down while laboring

on his Cambridge prairie.
These tools of mine—rusty scythe

and rickety hayrake—are quaint
artifacts suburbanites buy

at antique shops and garage sales
to adorn basement dens.

I pray with each swing:
let me die here rather

than suffer a like fate
(to the tools I mean).

Let me lie here—near this lazy
creek—with owl and whippoorwill

to sing at my wake
and deer and woodchuck to sniff

my grave. There is no place
else I crave to go.

Crows

A silence and stillness
that seems almost sacred
pervades this place
most of the time, but now,
just before dusk,
the quiet is shattered
by the invasion
of a legion of crows.

They storm into the pines,
twenty or more of them,
a boisterous black rabble
flying from tree to tree
raising a holy ruckus.

As I attempt to walk up
into the woods, gain
a better vantage from which
to watch their plotting,
they fly off in a squawking
flurry, then settle a hundred feet
away, a belligerent mob
refusing to disperse.

They are the fallen angels,
organized now, preparing
to assail the gates of heaven.

Picking Apples

My cash reserves running low,
I hired on picking apples.
The orientation was simple and terse:
"Pull up on the apple and it will snap off"
and "don't let them fall".

Of course, plenty fell as I struggled
to position the gangling ladder
in the tree, and more as I stretched
for a full branch of apples that seemed,
like paradise, always just out of reach.

Balanced precariously in the flimsy branches,
hanging by a prayer, I snatched each apple
and dropped it in my canvas satchel.
When it was full, I made the slow descent
and dumped my bounty in a wooden crate.

Bored, I sought amusement in mind games,
wondering which might be that mythic tree
promising knowledge of good and evil
with one bite of its bright red flesh.

But too late, I thought, and then the game
was spoiled. I've seen some good
in my time, and have known a lot of evil.
But being innocent was not much fun.
A little sin has done me a world
of good. And another apple falls.

The Butterfly Does Yoga

A beautiful day,
sunny and mild.
I take a blanket outdoors
to stretch my limbs
and joints, stiff and sore
from picking apples.

A little russet-colored
butterfly flutters by
and alights on my bare toes.
It clings there the entire time
as I work my way through
the triangle, tree, mountain
and warrior poses.

It is a meadow fritillary.
The adult feeds
on nectar and dung.
Which flavor, I wonder,
are my toes?

November Woods

The woods are bare
and still and every
creature that harbors

hope to live another
year has gone in
search of hollowed

trees or caves or
coverts or else
has burrowed

underground, and
in the distance
I hear the thunder

of hunter's guns
spending their practice
rounds, for their time

is near, and here,
even the tiny
nuthatch, poking

at this tree and
that, does not dawdle,
heedful that time

will not wait.
A few lonely
oak leaves are all

that remain above,
swaying stubbornly
in the autumn

breeze like beggars
at street corners
refusing to

admit defeat,
but underfoot,
amidst brown duff

and dying debris,
a patch of bright
green lichen

on a stone, plucky
wild ginger and
a few fern fronds,

the taunting green
more mockery
than promise, like

a young woman
flirting
with an old man.

Government in a Box

Cold Day in November

The morning paper reports it's changing
of the guard but what is there left to guard
I want to know while outside the window
birds are building a nest in the sill
where the air conditioner still sits
that I had every intention of removing
before winter sets in and the birds
are making conversation and I want to ask
what they know that I don't what secrets
they might be privy to and shouldn't they
be flying south or to another country
but I fail to decipher even one word
they are saying as they sally back and forth
between window and cedar trees. I can't
imagine they are discussing the new guard
and whether it will be better or worse
than the old and whether any bird
should give a flying fuck and whither went
the drone of the air conditioner and in truth
I don't even know what kind of birds
these are I think I'll just call them juncos.

The Real Story

No, not meek and mild, like
the cards and carols claim. No,
not *this* child. I swear he came,
not whimpering but howling wild
like a wolf or the northwest wind.
No gold halo like a ring
around a planet to grace a beatific
smile. Rather, a dark face
already stained with joy and doubt,
hints of anguish, betrayal, and pain
to come, hair damp and matted
like the sheep that strayed here
this dark night, not lured
by angel's hymns but by a cry
so fierce and full of life
and fury that they know in their woolly
sheep hearts that this will be
the blackest lamb of all, this wild
unruly child who will refuse to hearken
to the call of kings or priests
or even fathers, instead to follow
a distant and lonely star.

My God is Greater Than Your God

but I haven't
just yet
figured out exactly
who he or she is
though I'm working
on it and I swear
I love my sports teams
as much as anyone
but when the boy-man
crosses himself
at the free-throw line
or genuflects in self-less
praise after catching
the touchdown pass, I turn
away from the TV

and when the boy-men pray
with their platoon leader or
chaplain before marching
off to another war
I wonder who is this god
who bothers
to pick sides
and bestow a blessing
on what they are about
to do, and then

there are those times
that some, claiming
to be believers, condemn
and cry out *heathen*
because their own puny god
loves guns or hates gays
or thinks sex is only
for the married, or else
their god
(or so they claim)
has set the banquet table
for their members only

and I'd like to say: *If your god
is so great, then how come
your heaven's so small?*

but instead I'm wishing
I could feel the same conviction
and passion as they do
for my own god who
even in my deepest darkest
doubting moments I know must
encompass this whole sparkling
and dreadfully mysterious
universe, its fifty billion galaxies
and every lonely lost star,
even those now mere embers
that burned bright
with savage fury
just a billion years ago.

Young Americans Dressed in Black

for Paul Goodman

I wish to see the streets swell
with these earnest Americans, knowing
full well that the larger the crowd,
the more alone I will feel.

Today I stand in the shadows watching
the young ones dressed in black,
their ragged black flag fluttering
in February's breeze, as they march by

beating on plastic buckets like bratty children.
I am old enough to be their father
and would not expect them to invite
me inside their clubhouse, even if I dared

ask, but my dark and brooding heart
heaves with joy to see them break ranks
and spoil the neat plans of my friends,
who want only to hand themselves over,

politely, to the police and be led away
in quiet pairs without having bothered
to disturb the peace. In this country
that is not mine, these young Americans

dressed in black are the nearest thing
to beauty that I know, yet I will put on
a tie when I mean to make trouble,
resigned to never know how they come by

their brand of anarchism, and they will never
know my father Goodman who, like me,
often stood sulking in these shadows,
watching the young and pretty ones,

wishing only to be of use, hungering
for a home in this alien world,

wanting only to sew and fly a simple flag
with no colors that no one need salute.

El Fuego

Once the biggest slash pile was blazing,
so bold and beautiful, Pablo,
at the cabin by the Kickapoo,
I grabbed your book from the outhouse,
the one that had sat there twenty years
or more—docile as a peasant—with only
the mice paying it any mind.
It was nine o'clock sharp, the start

of spring, and I was impatient to be rid
of everything old—or dead cold—so I
opened your musty book to the poem
you called *El Fuego* and read a few lines
to the ear of flames, then tossed it on the bonfire
while it was at its glorious zenith.
I hesitate to say it was meant as absolution

or consummation of anything I can name,
but it felt right to watch the flames
rise and flutter like butterflies, the ground
scorched and charred around me,
a harbinger of something new, and only then
I thought about how the fascists
had gathered your books from the homes

and libraries and heaped them on the pyres
in the streets of Santiago. The books
crackled in the flames like roasting flesh
but the words leapt from the page
and cried out in holy rage—like Joan of Arc,
Norman Morrison, or Buddhist monks
on fire in Vietnam. And the word was made

flesh, and the flesh
made word.

Government in a Box

We've got a government in a box, ready to roll in. —Gen. Stanley McChrystal, American commander in Afghanistan, February 2010

When the killing is nearly done
our government says
it's going to deliver
a brand-new government
in a box
for those pathetic people
who never had one
as good as ours.

But what kind of box, I wonder,
to hold a whole government?
A cardboard box?
As big as a breadbox
or small as a match box?
Toolbox? Safe-deposit box?
Shoe box? A wooden box,
made of boxwood, shaped
to look like a casket?

A ballot box? Lunch box?
Pandora's box?
Jack-in-the-box?
Perhaps a box within a box
within a box, like
Russian nesting dolls.

Will there be a bow on the box?
Will the box be wrapped
with bright tissue? Or just
brown butcher paper?

Will there be a key
to open the box?
Or a password or secret code
or written instructions in their
native tongue? Or will they
need to use box cutters?

And most important, who will
be chosen to open the box?
Who will choose the chosen?
Will there be killing?

Snapshots from Another Time

Snapshots from Another Time

snapshot: *a hurried shot fired with little or no aim; quick offhand shot.*

1.
A ragged notebook, stashed in a drawer.
Rolls of film, never used. Scraps of paper
with names and addresses in another language.
A phrase book. A bright clay dish for friends
to admire, to pass around the dinner table.
Shards of memory, souvenirs.

2.
¿Se puede sacar un foto, por favor?
Fingers numb on the dumb metal shutter.
Phrases and faces to commit to memory.
A few hurried lines, nearly illegible,
like messages smuggled by spies
across enemy lines. Keepsakes.

*¿Se puede sacar un foto, por favor? No,
tengo miedo.*

3.
Back again in the bloated belly of the beast,
confronted by choices but nothing worth doing.
That is my excuse to you. It is much harder,
here, to play the hero. Not like you, who have
no choice but to be a heroine. All my life
I've made choices by *not* choosing.
Now I not-choose again, to let you go.

4.
No light to penetrate the black box, to strike
the film fretting like a dark virgin.
Just one hasty shot of Rafael, his black hair

flowing past his shoulders, magnificent mustache,
two crosses draped from his neck.
Rafael, who opened wide his two hands
to prove he was a worker, not guerrilla,
and still they poured salt water in his wounds,

hit him with a hammer and knocked him
senseless three times in one hour.

Salt in his wounds.

¿Se puede sacar un foto?
No, por favor. Es peligroso.

5.
It can be explained with science, by someone
who knows such things. A suspension of salt
of silver in gelatin and then a series
of chemical interactions…

Always in the darkroom, a mysterious
and miraculous moment when the image
first materializes in the tray.
Then there is clarity; the choices are easy.

6.
No photo of your face. No passages
in the notebook to implicate you. Nothing
to remind me it was not a dream,
dancing all night in a disco in Bogotá.
Sipping Cokes and eating hamburgers
while soldiers searched people
in the street below.

¿Un foto, por favor?
No, es peligroso.

7.
Just one quick shot of Sister Libia,
on the playground, soccer ball in her hands,
niños huddled around her. Sister Libia,
teaching at Santa Rita, high in the hills
of the barrio above Medellin. Sister Libia,
who took the gun from the muchacho
every morning when he came to school,
tucked it snug as a sleeping child
in the file cabinet
beside the report cards, and dutifully

returned it when the school bell rang,
until the morning
he came no more,
found the next day, a bullet in his head.

Dead.

¿Se puede sacar un foto?

8.
Long ago I had a friend who believed
he could summon magic like a genie
from the black box. Later
he gave away the camera, tried to find
the magic in a bottle, and went out west
and drank himself to death.

9.
No, por favor. Es peligroso.

A pity. No picture. How I waited
that last morning, hoping you would come.
Wanting time for one photo
so later I would not think
you had been a dream.

¿Por favor, se puede sacar un foto?

10.
No, lo siento. ¡Es muy peligroso!

No picture of Pedro, forced to march
his seven-year-old son with a hood
over his head. His two daughters already dead.
His neighbor, a catechist, killed
and dressed to look like the guerrilla.

¿Se puede sacar un foto?

11.
No, por favor. Es peligroso.

No photo of the young men
in jail in Barranca, the ones who gave us
fruit juice and chairs and sat calmly
on their white cots telling their stories.
How they were picked off the streets
and brought to the barracks and beaten.
Yet how gentle they were
with each other, with us.

12.
Claro que no. No foto.

No photo of you and the other
young ones (and the Jesuit with a bounty
on his head, a bulls-eye on his back)
huddled together in an upper room
around a plain wood table.
A book and cup of wine. Wind howling
and wailing outside. Even I, the doubting one,
felt the spirit pour forth
as the wine was passed
and wondered if this was that thing
some call God.

13.
Nada. No importa.

A pity. No picture of the poor peasant
cutting bananas when the paramilitary
came, insisting he knew
where the guerrilla was, and swore:
*We are going to see you
with your mouth full of flies.*

¿Se puede sacar un foto?

14.
No, lo siento. No photo.
Es muy peligroso. Riding in a cab
high above the noise and lights of Bogotá,
wanting to say something with my scraps

of broken Spanish, knowing even English
could not suffice.

15.
¡No, es peligroso!

No light to pierce the film
waiting patient as a peasant in the magic box.
Like a secret in a dark heart. Shadows
on an alley wall.

16.
Months later, in the mail, a photo
the size of a postage stamp.

A keepsake. Keep safe.

When you wrote *te querido*, I had to thumb
through the phrasebook, not knowing if this
was just a way of speaking. As if I were
to say I *loved* this scarred, brutalized,
beautiful land of yours. So much is lost.
Translation, after all.

Lo siento.

# The Devil's Grandmother

If I Had Gone to Church

this Sunday morning, I would not
have heard Allen reciting Howl and Kaddish
on the radio, would not have seen
the silky white cat slink
through the shrubs stalking God-knows-what,
would not have recalled how the poet sat
cross-legged on the bare-wood living room
floor of our flat in Milwaukee playing
the harmonium, how he chuckled
when I put Cat Stevens on the turntable—
at the part where *Mary dropped her pants
by the sand and let a parson come
and take her hand*—would not have seen
the hummingbird hover two feet
in front of my face as I sat on the garden swing,
or smelled the honeysuckle, nor heard
the sandhill cranes chortling high in the sky
above, would not have savored the dark roast
coffee so exquisite with the huckleberry buckle
baked last night with berries from the garden.
      What would I have done in church
except pretend—in deference to all those
Sunday seekers—to be nearer there than here
to what is all around me, spread out
for those with eyes to see, like a holy banquet
upon the earth, this kingdom coming now
right now this Sunday morning.

Leftovers

After the Thanksgiving dinner,
we brought leftover turkey home.

As usual. The first night we fixed
turkey fried rice, turkey tostadas the next,

and a pot of turkey soup after that.
The homemade whipped cream, left over

from the pumpkin pie, we dropped
in great dollops in our coffee

each morning. It was *awesome*.
It must be thirty years since

I first heard that word, when we arrived
at my sister's home in the suburbs

with real whipping cream, not the stuff
in a spray can, and my young nephew Davey

watched in wonder while I whipped it up
in a cold bowl and he exclaimed: awesome.

It's twelve years now since
the car crash and I've heard that word

at least a million times. You can say
something or do something so often

that it loses all meaning. But sometimes,
like loaves and fishes, and baskets

full of leftovers after the motley multitude
of seekers has been fed, or prayers recited

by rote on a holy day, if you look
or listen carefully, you can catch a spark

of miracle in the mundane, in the simple
multiplicity of a word a child utters

or the simple act of sitting together at table
each year, eating in memory of one

who came and left, so suddenly,
so utterly.

Table Manners

You grab your plate and retreat
inside to eat alone, angry
with me for suggesting that talking
and listening are separate actions
that can't possibly be done
simultaneously.
(Not to mention eating too).

Then I remember my father
lecturing us children not to talk
with food in our mouths and I worry
that I might be becoming like him.

But look! Here come the boisterous
Cedar Waxwings—returning again
as each September—to plunder
the red cedar trees and feast
on the diminutive slate-gray berries.

Now you return too, plate in hand.
Perhaps the birds have called
you out of yourself, and me from my
darker crow-like querulousness.
They are rambunctious, full of high
spirits, garrulous too, as they strip
the trees of their fruit.

They carouse joyfully, grateful
for this blessed back-yard providence.
They care not who is saying what
or why and who spoke first
and which one is talking
with a mouthful of berries.

In the English Language There Is Only One Word for Dream

We are playing tennis in the basement
of the house we had walked away from,

the house that was ours no more, you going
back to the city, me: where? But here we are,

swatting the ball back and forth, intense
and agile. At one point, I push an old sofa

out of the way and the flurry of volleys
persists. There is no net between us.

I hit the ball at you in a fury
and then it morphs into a butterfly

and I'm sleeping restlessly, this night after
the doctors have unclogged, once more,

the pathway to my heart. This heart, battered
but still beating, sucking in blood, flushing it out,

and now the sweet breath of another day as the ball,
wings aflutter, floats away, and I can't

remember if we are keeping score
and what part love plays.

Leaving the Garden

You knew this day would come,
didn't you? Turning over the soil
for the last time, remembering
routines that never seemed routine.
The double-digging a decade
or more ago, the soil never the same:
too moist, too dry, at times just right.

How you turned it over and tucked
the voracious earthworms back in,
recalling once more that it's just
a myth how they heal miraculously
when sliced in half with the shovel,
and now you hear your heart insist
no creature can expect ever to be whole
again after losing something so precious.

How you tossed the stones and walnut
shells on the path, and here you are,
still fishing rusty nails and shards
of glass out of the dirt, stuffing them
in the back pocket of your jeans.
All the shovelsful of compost, peat
and manure you sprinkled in the beds
while robins waited patiently nearby,
knowing there would be worms for lunch.

Sometimes a toad was exposed
and you sent him on his way with a nudge
of your finger. Once you uncovered
a nest of baby rabbits. One of them,
too small or scared to move, huddled
there all night on the garden path.
In the morning, you watched a crow
swoop down and carry it off.

The cedar waxwings came again
last month, gorging themselves on berries
of the red cedars with no thought
that providence might ever fail to provide.

And the resurrection lilies by the pond
rose once more, out of the dark, in a burst
of glory, and you marveled at their blind faith.

Now it's late October, still warm,
and the birch trees are clinging
tenaciously to their last few leaves.
Your greenhouse is gone now,
just a dark blemish on the ground
where it once sat. A would-be farmer
with dreams of plump red tomatoes
hauled it away, battered though it was
from the time the storm snatched it up
and tossed it on its side.

Hastily you harvest a few beets and carrots
and leave the rest in the ground–soon
to be frozen–recalling the years of labor,
the love once fresh, now wilted.
A mother of the new couple comes
to inspect the house and eyes the vase
of flowers on the kitchen counter,
vibrant purple coneflowers and
black-eyed susans from the garden,
and she hands them to you, saying
"They won't be needing this."

How can she say what they might need?
you think, but you take them, a bittersweet
gift for the first person you meet
on the street, because it hurts too much
to hold on to them, and you walk out,
you walk away, and don't look back.

After Reading the First Poem in the Literary Journal, I Stop to Contemplate Life and Death

It was a good strong poem. About how someone
had died and all his friends had gathered at the pub

to ponder his passing and that time-worn mystery
of where we all go when we are gone. The world

is turning towards spring as I flip to the back

of the journal to peruse the listing of publications,
awards and brief bio. But the poet is past tense.

He died of cancer in November, never saw in print
this good strong poem about him and friends drinking

to the memory of their deceased companion.

Next week I start a new job, my first 9-to-5 in decades.
For years now, the days have been rushing by like…

well, the newly-dead poet said it best: *like bats at dusk.*
The way they whoosh across the darkening sky,

webbed wing-hands fluttering too fast to see.

Each day I make a list of things to do and at day's end,
to my disgust, I've checked off just a few. Now here,

mocking me in this pile of unread magazines,
the latest issue of *AARP*, (did I subscribe?) with the

cover story: *Find a New Job: Make Yourself Relevant.*

I'd like to think I had been, but now I'm wondering
if the dead poet, had he known he wouldn't live

to see this last poem published, might have chosen
a different piece to go out with, perhaps one about ice

cracking on a creek in spring, chickadees chirping

in the morning, the first blush of green on a lilac shrub
or a crocus pushing its nose through snow, rather than this

good strong poem about him and his buddies drinking
to a friend's demise, wondering where we go when we leave

here, what's on the other side of life, and those bats at dusk.

The Devil's Grandmother

For the godzillionth time today
I'm about to feel sorry for myself,
realizing how little you understand me
(or how little any of those other lovers
did either) when I pause to ponder
the inexplicable miracle
that they all loved me anyway
(at least for a while), in spite of that lack
of knowledge, or perhaps *because* of it,
and then I recall how Nora Barnacle confessed
to Joyce before he died that she hadn't actually
read any of his books (maybe she would
someday, after he was gone), and how
she once said *Ulysses* was *swinish*,
(even though she hadn't read it) and how,
when Carl Jung wrote Joyce to praise
his writing, saying he knew more about women
than *the devil's grandmother*, Nora scoffed,
saying *He knows nothing at all about women!*
And, in spite of all that, Joyce had written
this book set on the day he met her,
and later *Bloomsday* became a national holiday
(even though it was only fiction), and then
it struck me that having a woman *understand*
you need not be a criteria for loving her
(or her you), even if she's never read
your books or one miserable poem or your mind
or your damn dreams, so what the hell, I swear
on my own grandmother's grave, if love
could be understood or explained, it probably
wouldn't exist, so I declare right here and now
that the day we met (do you remember when
that was?) should be proclaimed a national holiday,
but that's something you can work on
after I'm dead, my dear. Let's just enjoy
each other for today.

About the Author

Tom Boswell is a poet, freelance journalist, photographer and community organizer residing in Madison, Wisconsin. His work has appeared in *Atlanta Review*, *Rattle*, *Poet Lore*, *Rosebud*, *Two Thirds North*, the *Lascaux Prize* and other journals, as well as the anthologies *New Poetry from the Midwest* and *Local News: Poetry About Small Towns*.

He has won national competitions judged by Tony Hoagland, Luis Alberto Urrea, and Robert Cording. His first chapbook, *Midwestern Heart*, was published by Codhill Press in 2012. His second, *Neighbors*, was published by Evening Street Press in 2018.